SONG
of a Prisoner

SONG
of a Prisoner

OKOT p'BITEK

Introduction by Edward Blishen, B.B.C.
Illustrations by E. Okechukwu Odita

THE THIRD PRESS
Joseph Okpaku Publishing Company, Inc.
444 Central Park West, New York, N.Y. 10025

First Printing

Copyright © 1971 by Okot p'Bitek

All rights reserved. Except for use in a review, the reproduction or utilization of this work or part of it in any form or by electronics, or other means, now known or hereafter invented, including xerography, photocopying, and recording, and any information storage and retrieval system is forbidden without the written permission of the publisher.

Library of Congress Catalogue Card Number: 77-148363

SBN: Cloth 89388-004-3
Paper 89388-005-1

Printed in the U.S.A.

Designed by Barbara Kohn Isaac

for
lumumba mondale kimathi mboya tshombe balewa . . .
    none of whom
    will ever read it

    and for the
    bruised others . . .

Contents

	Introduction	1
1.	Dung of Chicken	41
2.	Wounded Crocodile	49
3.	Black Mud	53
4.	Bonfire	59
5.	Sacred Rock	63
6.	This Stupid Bitch	69
7.	Voice of a Dove	73
8.	Distant Echoes	78
9.	Jubilant Throng	83
10.	Killer Mark	87
11.	Soft Grass	91
12.	Youthful Air	99
13.	Cattle Egret	105
14.	Oasis	111
15.	Undergrowth	115

Introduction

We are desperately close to the birth of a modern literature, especially in English, in the newly independent countries of East Africa. It seems only yesterday (and indeed it *was* only yesterday) that a common theme of discussion was the slowness of Kenyans, Ugandans, Tanzanians to produce such a literature, as compared with the gush of urgency that marked the appearance of novels, plays, poems in West Africa. That discussion has become, in no time at all, queerly academic. Within the space of a few years, East Africa has discovered a wide range of remarkable voices: and none is more remarkable, more enigmatic and more the subject of controversy, than that of Okot p'Bitek, an Acholi from Uganda.

I say we are "desperately close" because it is obviously difficult to achieve anything like perspective in however tentative a judgement on the new East African literature. A critic is like some early map-maker: he must fill the blanks with whales and dolphins. He must hint at the possibility of a coastline, rather than suggest that he really knows its configuration. Yet there are great and legitimate excitements in such a moment in the growth of a human enterprise, when so much is doubtful. And one of the excitements comes, when it is literature we are concerned with, from the early appearance of a figure so clearly extraordinary as Okot p'Bitek. If the world lasts, and our children are at length able to begin to fill in this literary map with ordinary critical confidence, it is certain that they will not draw the outlines of his work and his significance as we must do it now—first map-makers as we are. But I'm quite sure he will not have vanished from the map altogether, or have been swallowed by a whale or dolphin. By any standards, and making all the necessary allowances for an over-close viewpoint, he is astonishing and important both as a person and as a writer.

The biographical facts are themselves remarkable. He was born in 1931 at Gulu in Northern Uganda, and was educated first at Gulu High School and later at one of the most high-flying of Ugandan schools, King's College, Budo. He went on to read education at Bristol, law at Aberystwyth and social anthropology at Oxford: returning to Uganda, he lectured at the University College at Makerere. This academic versatility was matched by considerable athletic skill: among other achievements, he played football for Uganda. A drummer and dancer, he founded an annual festival of African arts at Gulu. For a while he was Director of the National Cultural Centre in Kampala. His first published work—a novel, *Lak Tar,* written in Lwo—appeared when he was only twenty-two. A class-mate of his, the equally vivid Taban lo Liyong (on whose opinions any critic must draw heavily at this stage), believes that Okot was already, in the 1950s, at work on a long poem which did not appear until 1966, and which at once established Okot's reputation beyond the boundaries of Uganda and indeed far beyond Africa. This poem, in Okot's own English translation known as *Song of Lawino,* caused an instant stir.

But before I look at that poem, let me say what little I am able to, about the author himself. I think only a fellow-Ugandan could draw a reliable portrait of him: and even such an observer might have difficulty with so complicated and mischievous a sitter. His mischievous high spirits, indeed, are an aspect of the man that must strike anyone at a first meeting. I encountered him shortly after the publication of *Lawino,* early in 1967. Okot is explosive, elusive . . . many obvious words rush into the mind: dynamic, awkward, witty . . . I found myself thinking of him as a Byronic figure: absurd enough, I suppose, as an analogy, and yet there is much that suggests it—the overnight fame brought about by a single poem, the talent for irony and satire, the clearly brilliant gift, the quality of the *enfant terrible.* He explodes incessantly—into laughter powerful enough, drawn sufficiently from the belly, to make a decorous Englishman like myself, especially in otherwise formal surroundings, look nervously over his shoulder. I hope I have indicated that Okot is in no sense a conventional person. When I said goodbye to him, in the square in front of the National Cultural Centre in Kampala, he subjected me to a dramatic embrace—

over one shoulder, and then over the other. Then his great laugh crashed out. The salutation was genuine enough, as I later reasoned when, somewhat bruised, I boarded the aeroplane for London. But I'm certain that Okot enjoyed the idea of departing so far from an Englishman's expectations in the matter of a farewell embrace. He knew I should have been much more at home with a handshake. He delighted in the unpliant astonishment with which I lent myself to these valedictory acrobatics.

A trivial story: but I think it is not possible to understand Okot p'Bitek's work without being aware of his vast appetite for teasing. Taban lo Liyong finds too much of the jester in *Song of Lawino*. But this is a jester whose gaiety is often fanged. When I was in Kampala, Okot had just taken over the directorship of the National Cultural Centre. He found it the haunt of expatriate dramatic societies, performing Noel Coward, Terence Rattigan. Okot announced that he meant to make the Centre's work truly African. This would mean that he must have more room than was then available for the storing of his African costumes, masks, musical instruments and other properties. Part of the Centre was occupied at the time by the British Council, under an arrangement, as I gathered, that had its roots in a contribution made by the Council to the building of the Centre. The British Council clearly brought out all the mischief in Okot—which was not wholly light-hearted. He certainly wanted that extra space: but he wanted also to cause a merry disturbance. A dispute, of a kind he clearly delights in, gathered head. There were occasions when Okot exaggerated or even invented the case made by his enemy, so that he might demolish it the more wittily. I don't think anyone in the British Council in Kampala actually maintained that the piano was the national instrument of Uganda. But Okot pretended that this claim had been made. The piano must go, and all it stood for. "The national instrument of Uganda," he roared in the public press, "is the drum. Not tinkle, tinkle, tinkle—but drum, drum, drum!" I may have misremembered his words slightly, but that was the gist of them. I certainly remember him crying "Drum, drum, drum!" in a reverberant whisper, at a party made delightfully uneasy by the dispute. I remember also standing in the British Council offices and looking out at the grass plot in front of the Centre and observing a scene that had a comical quality of ominousness. Okot and some friends were busy planting and raising an immense pole in the middle of the green. There seemed, for one wild and thrilling moment, the possibility that it was a kind of gallows. Okot's enemies would die there —of course, in an atmosphere of laughter, dance and drumming. I am certain that Okot himself enjoyed that moment of ambiguity. The pole was, in fact, a drum pole round which he intended there should be dancing, as there is dancing round such poles in the Ugandan villages. But—did anyone tremble in the moments before this harmless purpose was revealed?

A party was given in the Centre to celebrate the publication of *Lawino*. Among my companions was

Richard Hughes, the distinguished novelist, to whom, as to me, the discovery of this poem was the outstanding literary experience of this visit to East Africa. At one point in the evening Mr. Hughes asked Okot if he would give us the particular pleasure of reading us a little of *Lawino*. It was clear to us that, above all, it was a poem to be listened to; and I think we both wanted to remember it in terms of Okot's own voice. The poet agreed and we withdrew to one side. There was music and dancing almost everywhere in the crowded foyer of the Centre, but we found a tiny patch of relative silence and Okot began reading. I still hear his voice in my ears when I turn the pages of the poem. It was a light, throwaway voice that moved over the words softly, mischievously, with occasional sudden stabs of anger—sudden rises to a high pitch of mockery—and sudden telling descents which made the most of the poem's passages of irony. Though when I say "passages" I am reminded of one of the chief qualities of *Lawino* made clear to me by that memorable reading: that though it does have its sustained passages, seemingly marked by single moods, it is, in fact, and largely, a poem of considerable subtlety. The apparent single moods are woven of many strands of feeling: it must be read like a dramatic soliloquy, with much variation of tone, manner, weight. Within that very quiet reading of Okot's, in the National Cultural Centre that evening, there was this great variety of nuance, which made me even more aware than I had been that the voice of the poem is a most complicatedly and convincingly *living* voice.

Lawino is, among other things, a fine dramatic set piece.

I remember that when the reading was over and we rejoined the party, I passed a visiting academic, a highly intelligent critic of generally radical views, who murmured: "Oh, it is trying to set the clock back! *Lawino* is simply trying to put back the clock!" It was said, as I recall, quite desperately: here was a critic who clearly felt, in that atmosphere of congratulation and admiration, that someone had to say: All right—but it's a very dangerous poem, y'know! It's very wrong-headed and anyone who takes it seriously is going to be badly misled!

And *Lawino* has been the centre of the sort of controversy this troubled academic hinted at, ever since it appeared. Except here and there under Taban lo Liyong's affectionately fierce scrutiny,[1] it is never attacked for lack of literary skill. A recent critic, Okumu pa'Lukubo—also Ugandan, and made uneasy, much as lo Liyong is, by the assumptions and apparent claims made by the poem—hastens to assert his admiration for the power with which *Lawino* is written.[2] But the poem, as perhaps few have ever done, divides its readers on a single, startling issue. Entangled in the poem are that generous instinct for mischief that I have suggested is of more than ordinary importance in Okot p'Bitek's makeup; a satirical energy that

---
[1] *Lawino is Unedu*: in *The Last Word* (East African Publishing House, 1969).
[2] Review of *Lawino* in *Nanga,* May 1970 (National Teachers' College, Kyambogo, Uganda).

sometimes allows the pure fun of an idea to run away with the poet; and a deep, awkward, important argument that in some respects is perhaps not yet ready for wholly rational discussion, and in other respects perhaps lies deeper than such discussion. The light-voiced quality of *Lawino,* and its long stretches of malicious gaiety, can, I have come to believe, seriously mislead a critic, and cause him to look elsewhere than in the proper place for the poem's importance.

Song of Lawino, A Lament is a poem in thirteen parts. It was translated into English from the Acholi by the author who states that he "has thus clipped a bit of the eagle's wings and rendered the sharp edges of the warrior's sword rusty and blunt, and has also murdered rhythm and rhyme." As to this, I can only say that the eagle's wings must originally have been of quite terrifying span, and the warrior's sword dazzlingly sharp and shining. As to rhyme, the loss of it has led, in English, to a curiously exciting pace which, as we have the poem, might cause any reader to feel that rhyme would act as an unwelcome brake. The rhythm, in English, is most subtle and flowing.

Taban lo Liyong is convinced that *Lawino* is the final form of a poem Okot was working on in 1954, when it had some such title as *Te Okono pe Luputu*—"positively translatable," says lo Liyong, "as: Respect the Ways of Your People, or Stick to Acholi Customs, or Blackman, be Proud of African Traditions—and Don't Abandon Them for the Whiteman's." Any of these titles certainly sums up the apparent statement the poem makes. The argument is put into the bitter mouth of the wife of Ocol, a chief's son, who has thrown her aside in favour of "a modern girl." The dominant tone of Lawino's comment on her rival can be illustrated from her first discussion of "the beautiful one," whose name is Clementine.

> Brother, when you see Clementine!
> The beautiful one aspires
> To look like a white woman;
>
> Her lips are red-hot
> Like glowing charcoal,
> She resembles the wild cat
> That has dipped its mouth in blood,
> Her mouth is like raw yaws,
> It looks like an open ulcer,
> Like the mouth of a fiend!
> Tina dusts powder on her face
> And it looks so pale . . .

This is the manner, widely throughout the poem. The tone is, on the surface, one of naive astonishment. Lawino is almost tenderly bemused by Tina's makeup, as she is by Ocol's preference for English over his mother tongue, for books over dancing; and, when it comes to dancing, for Western forms rather than Ugandan ones. But there's no tenderness here, of course. In his reading, to Richard Hughes and me, Okot's tone in such a passage had the quality of a kind of surprised purring, but it was not the purring of a domestic cat. Intense savagery lies under this surface, and never more so than when Lawino is pretending to be reasonable. To me, part of the comic force of the poem lies in the frequent conflict between the tone and the actual words that Lawino speaks: and one of Okot's great skills in writing it, certainly in this translation, lies in his having so laid out the poem that, inevitably, one registers this clash of manner and content.

Setting out her case in the opening section of the poem, Lawino inveighs against her husband's distaste for her, her relatives and his own clansmen. She is, according to Ocol, unlettered, unbaptised (and so no better than a dog), primitive. She is at fault because she cannot play the guitar or count coins. She is silly. Her mother is a witch: her clansmen are fools "because they eat rats." All of them are sorcerers. Indeed, all black people are primitive, and "their ways are utterly harmful."

> Ocol says he is a modern man,
> A progressive and civilised man,
> He says he has read extensively and widely
> And he can no longer live with a thing like me
> Who cannot distinguish between good and bad.

Alongside this report of Ocol's opinions, Lawino chides him, in terms that are to grow stronger as the poem continues. He is not a man any longer—he is a dead fruit! He is behaving like a child! His people, she hints, make up songs of ridicule about him—he who, as son of a Chief, should be the subject of songs of praise.

Then follows the attack on Clementine. This has, at times, a feline hilarity: the claws scratch deep.

> And when she walks
> You hear her bones rattling.
> Her waist resembles that of the hornet.

But suddenly the note changes. There are passages in this poem, when Lawino celebrates the customs of her own people, that have a quality of elation—limpid, lyrical—and also of great gravity that are most deeply moving. So here, at the end of her tooth-and-nail attack on her rival, Lawino is made to speak of the Acholi woman's traditional attitude to her husband's need of other women.

> I am not unfair to my husband.
> I do not complain
> Because he wants another woman,
> Whether she is young or aged!
> Who has ever prevented men
> From wanting women?

Jealousy is a weakness—it can only mean that a woman is aware of her own defects. The competition for a man's love is a fair one, conducted according to perfectly reasonable rules.

> You win him with a hot bath
> And sour porridge.
> The wife who brings her meal first,
> Whose food is good to eat . . .
> Such is the woman who becomes
> The head-dress keeper.

She has no fear of competing with Clementine, Lawino claims. What she asks is that her husband should cease insulting her, and should recognise that the ways of his ancestors are good:

> Their customs are solid,
> And not hollow,
> They are not thin, not easily breakable,
> They cannot be blown away
> By the winds
> Because their roots reach deep into the soil.

And Lawino goes on to make an important statement —important, that is, because it has so often been said, carelessly, that *Song of Lawino* is simply an attack on the Western way of life.

> I do not understand
> The ways of foreigners,
> But I do not despise their customs.
> Why should you despise yours?

It is still possible, taking this passage into account, to claim (as lo Liyong does) that the poem is a hopeless plea for the cessation of all cultural borrowing: that the Acholi customs themselves have no particular purity in this respect: and that indeed many of the customs celebrated by Lawino had fallen into disuse by the time the poem was written. But I believe it is essential to note that Lawino is not crying out against imported practices because those practices are in themselves detestable. She is rather trying to preserve a dream of, as it were, coherent cultural habit. The argument, as an argument, is so vulnerable (thus Okumu pa'Lukubo can point out that Acholi women are themselves great users of cosmetics, and that the great Acholi dances have become museum-pieces) that, given so plainly intelligent a poet, we have to look, I believe, below the surface for what is really being said. Given also the lyrical beauty of many of the passages in which Lawino speaks of Acholi customs. In a way, one could say this of the poem: that the intense longing for cultural coherence that arises from such passages is the *point* of the poem. It may be true that we cannot halt the dislocation of cultures that everywhere is occurring; or it may simply be true, as the poem seems often to imply, that the price paid for such dislocation is too high. But in fact it is an apparently impossible thing that is being said in *Song of Lawino*: that perhaps we should pause, or that perhaps we cannot afford to move at such a fantastic pace. This is impossible, as a statement, because we have nowhere in the world really begun to think along such lines. But in the impossible propositions set out by a poet have often lain the seeds of what, belatedly, the world has seen to be necessary kinds of action. *Lawino,* I suspect, is a poem that performs this function. We may swarm critically all over it, and point to all its logical weaknesses, and yet we may still not have robbed it of a fraction of its intrinsic strength. The poet, after all, is only describing his own sense of being himself intolerably divided. You can hardly study in three Western universities without becoming something of an Ocol, and yet we cannot doubt—I do not see how we can—that Lawino's voice is in great measure Okot's. It is in this sense that I mean that the argument may not yet be ready for wholly rational discussion. What appears to be an argument is often, I suggest, a simple statement of the poet's awareness of being divided against himself, and (as I think we shall see plainly when we turn to *Song of a Prisoner*) his awareness that the whole world is, in some such way, intolerably divided. I am often reminded, reading *Lawino,* of the great cry uttered, in so many and powerful ways, by the English poet John Donne as he stood with one foot in the medieval world and the other in the world of early modern science. Donne's arguments do not stand up: he cannot abolish the work of Copernicus: he cannot restore the medieval sense of a coherent chain of being. And yet his cry was essential to the awareness of his time. It was a cry that, under the hopelessness of the surface argument, was an utterly necessary reminder of the permanent human need of coherence, of order. And such a cry, I believe, *Lawino* utters: being, for that reason, a poem important not only to Africa, but to the whole world.

So, throughout much of the poem, a double operation is being conducted. All of Okot p'Bitek's deft and darting sense of mischief is at work when he attacks, in terms of Lawino's carefully wide-eyed and deceptively innocent amazement, the forms of dancing preferred by Ocol and Clementine: their Westernised taste in dress, their Western attitudes to time and to sickness and death. In much of this there is a marvellous, mischievous comedy. I have known Western readers bereft of all appetite for a while by Lawino's account of their feeding habits:

> The white man's stoves
> Are good for cooking
> White men's food:
> For cooking the tasteless
> Bloodless meat of cows
> That were killed many years ago
> And left in the ice
> To rot!
> For frying an egg
> Which when ready
> Is slimy like mucus,
>
> For boiling hairy chicken
> In saltless water.
> You think you are chewing paper!

Lo Liyong has curiously little patience with this element in the poem. It turns the work, he suggests, into "light literature" (a term which he surely ought to discuss before he uses it merely as a phrase of disparagement). "Too much space and energy," he argues, "is taken up with pointing out the foibles in the Western way of life . . . these foibles that are easily seen." Lo Liyong regards this as "childishness": "Some of it is fun for an Acholi audience: some impudence, some sarcasm, and plenty of 'raw' social anthropology. Juvenility. . . ." To say such things is surely to fail to weigh the pure comic success of these elements in the poem. It is not easy to imagine an Okot p'Bitek entirely or even largely stripped of his wicked and mocking manner. Even when he is most deeply serious, as we shall see when we look at *Song of a Prisoner,* a kind of dark laughter is never far away. And the truth is that much of *Lawino,* much that Okot's old classmate frowns over for its "lightness," has proved to be durable fun for audiences much wider and less special than Acholi ones. There is no wishing away the jester in this poet's work. When his targets are obvious, they are most unobviously teased and taunted.

The second part of the operation that one can see Okot conducting in *Lawino* lies in the account of Acholi customs and ways of life—idealised, no doubt, but not the less lovely and grave for all that. So, opposed to the hilariously mocking descriptions of Western dance is Lawino's celebration of Acholi dancing: to the tendentiously revolting view of the European *cuisine,* Lawino's marvellous tour of the Acholi kitchen:

> Here on your left
> Are the grinding stones:
> The big one
> Ashen and dusty
> And her daughter
> Sitting in her belly
> Are the destroyers of millet
> Mixed with cassava
> And sorghum.

It is all appallingly unfair, as lo Liyong notes—and yet again, one has to say that we are not really concerned with an attempt to be fair, to provide a balanced argument. It is with Western dance and cooking exactly as it was, in that dispute of Okot's with the British Council, with the piano. I remember that Okot made the piano, that patently superb musical instrument, seem an absurdity beneath one's contempt! How ridiculous the piano was! Not for one moment did one believe that Okot truly withheld his admiration from the piano: just as one would not have been surprised to see him dancing the detested rumba. This was not the sort of argument he was conducting. Mockery of the one was necessary to reinforce the idealisation of the other: of the piano, to promote the drum: of the rumba, to intensify the claims made for the get-stuck dance. Lo Liyong asks us to set on one side "all the crocodile tears which Okot made Lawino shed profusely, for Okot is a sceptic on the surface as well as between the lines." But for that sentence really to have meaning, lo

Liyong would have had to say that Okot was a *cynic*, not a sceptic: the claim being that he is making an empty show, in order to secure easy laughter and literary honour. Of course the surface of the work sparkles with scepticism, with all the facets of a complex and elusive mind. But I would argue that under this, there is the deepest possible gravity. And again, the test is one that each reader must make for himself, subjectively: it lies in the *tone* of what is written. I cannot doubt the profound seriousness of tone with which Okot addresses himself to the ways of the Acholi world. He may, for his own purpose, have turned that world into a Utopia. But to claim that he wrote these passages, so lyrically celebratory, with his tongue in his cheek, is (on the evidence of my ear) nonsense.

Another quality of Okot's writing to which I want to pay more attention when I come to *Song of a Prisoner* seems also, for what it implies as to the poet's entire intention, an element that can be weighed only by the ear, as it were—by the reader's general sensitiveness. It lies in that habit, so intrinsic to Okot p'Bitek's writing that one almost ceases to notice it, of referring incessantly to life other than human—to the life of animals, insects, plants.

> His eyes grow large,
> Deep black eyes,
> Ocol's eyes resemble those of the Nile Perch!
> He becomes fierce

Like a lioness with cubs,
He begins to behave like a mad hyena . . .

The backs of some books
Are hard like the rocky stem of the *poi* tree . . .

You wish you were lucky
To find someone to assist you
Who does not shout
Like house-flies
When disturbed
From an excreta heap! . . .

This is certainly a habit of Ugandan poetry, a deep part of the oral tradition. It is not an originality, in Okot. And yet it seems to me that his use of it, constant, profuse, is another means by which he roots his vision in Africa, and nowhere else: by which he brings the reader back, time and again, to that profound sense of place that, together with that profound sense of rooted custom he appears endlessly to offer as an alternative to the shallow confusions of half-westernised ways. Again, it is the rootedness he seems to insist upon. Again, under all the imperfections of the surface argument, what he can be felt to be saying is: Let us, before we enter the nowhereness of uniform modern existence, consider desperately the importance of knowing *where* we come from, *where* we live. Let us think generally in terms of roots. Or, to adapt the famous epigraph to the poem: Let us think what we shall be doing before we uproot the pumpkin in the old homestead. Lawino, in fact, is no innocent and naive village girl, at all. She is a poet and anthropologist, mingled, with a profoundly difficult and provocative argument to put forward in whatever ways may offer.

Of course, poets of any quality are mixed creatures! Of course, many of the criticisms that, in his lively way, Taban lo Liyong brings to bear against *Lawino*, and which really stem from his knowledge of Okot the man, are likely to be justified. Into Lawino's attacks on Western forms of religion lo Liyong reads Okot's malice towards the Catholic missions. No one can read this section without suspecting that personal revenges are being exacted. It is in this section and again in the section on politics, which lo Liyong feels to be the best in the poem, that Okot's impersonation of Lawino, the village girl, most obviously slips. The poet steps out from behind the mask. Without being experts on the Ugandan political situation, we can believe that, here and there, the voice that speaks is that of Okot p'Bitek, the disappointed political candidate. Lo Liyong says, from his knowledge of his friend, that if Okot has "an overriding passion beyond living life, it is politics." But when we have accepted that such a section of this poem, from a man so committed and concerned, so clearly and properly anxious to play a part in the developing history of his country, *must* have its moments when the frustrated or ordinarily irritated man speaks, rather than the larger poet, still, and especially in view of what is to come in *Song of a Prisoner,* one must note, and with proper gravity, what in essence is said in the eleventh part of *Song of Lawino*:

> If only the parties
> Would fight poverty
> With the fury
> With which they fight each other,
> If diseases and ignorance
> Were assaulted
> With the deadly vengeance
> With which Ocol assaults his mother's son,
> The enemies would have been
> Greatly reduced by now. . . .
>
> . . . those who have
> Fallen into things
> Throw themselves into soft beds,
> But the hip bones of the voters
> Grow painful
> Sleeping on the same earth
> They slept on
> Before Uhuru!

This does not belong to the field of purely personal revenges or irritations or disappointments. It is again a cry of something like panic at the rootless disorder of things—the too sudden and too infatuated plunge into some travesty of national politics.

I cannot leave *Lawino,* such a deviously serious poem, as I claim, and yet such a fiercely comic one, without a word about the twelfth part, called *My Husband's House is a Dark Forest of Books*. Here is

Okot p'Bitek, nourished on books, producer of books, in a wild extravaganza of disdain attacking Ocol for being a bookman. The section is worth looking at closely by any reader because it is so relevant to the accusation that, in much of the poem, Okot is intent purely on mischief, on appealing to the sense of fun of an Acholi audience. Whatever a reader's view about any argument for or against intellectualism, or bookishness, it would require a reader of some owlishness, and considerable resistance to comedy, not to be vastly entertained by this section.

> My husband's house
> Is a mighty forest of books,
> Dark it is and very damp,
> The steam rising from the ground
> Hot thick and poisonous
> Mingles with the corrosive dew
> And the rain drops
> That have collected in the leaves . . .
>
> For all our young men
> Were finished in the forest,
> Their manhood was finished
> In the classrooms,
> Their testicles
> Were smashed
> With large books!

Of course, one thinks with that radical academic, this is to put the clock back with a vengeance! Of course, one thinks momentarily with Lo Liyong, here is "Okot the sceptic posing as a champion for dying and dead customs he doesn't believe in." Here is Okot p'Bitek the intellectual pretending to a swinging anti-intellectualism! But one recovers quickly—I speak for myself—and adds two other statements. First: here is fun! Here is the most hilarious delight! If there had to be mockery of book-reading, could it be more amusingly, and more unexpectedly, expressed? in terms of a more grotesque poetry? And second: this cannot, in the nature of the poem and the poet, be merely mischief, or merely fun—or merely perversity! By an unbalanced bookishness, I think Okot is saying, it is possible that the new African is being severely damaged. Books have taken on an undue importance. Books have been resorted to beyond their true virtue. The use and reading of books, too, needs rooting in the African soil. The new man who tries to climb by books alone will climb nowhere at all.

Taban lo Liyong argued, in the essay already quoted, that *Song of Lawino* should be part of a triptych. Ocol should be allowed to state his case: so should Clementine. I don't know if it was in response to this suggestion that Okot wrote *Song of Ocol,* which appeared in 1970. It is a furious, headlong, bewildering poem, far briefer than *Lawino,* without the swarming life of its predecessor. I am indebted to my friend Cosmo Pieterse for the suggestion that, in this poem, Ocol is attempting to defend himself against accusations of which he has forgotten the actual nature. In the first five of its nine parts Ocol simply rages against old Africa. Lawino's song is

> the mad bragging
> Of a defeated general . . .

The whole past will be swept away. The pumpkin will go early—had already almost gone.

> I see a large pumpkin
> Rotting
> A thousand beetles
> In it;
> We will plough up
> All the valley,
> Make compost of the pumpkins
> And the other native vegetables,
> The fence dividing
> Family holdings
> Will be torn down,
> We will uproot
> The trees demarcating
> The land of clan from clan,
> We will obliterate
> Tribal boundaries
> And throttle native tongues
> To dumb death.

And this is the tone, this the wild and whirling character, of the first half of the poem. It is a destructive shout, close to hysteria. Old Africa is blisteringly impugned. All that Lawino celebrated is savaged by this extraordinary song of Ocol's. He cries out against the very fact of his Africanness.

> Mother, mother,
> Why,
> Why was I born
> Black?

All will be burned and broken. The whole past will be swept away: all the witches and wizards, the poets, priests, musicians, story tellers, myth makers, glorifiers of the past. There will be an end to

> The stupid village anthem of
> "Backward ever,
> Forwards never."

All the professors of anthropology and teachers of African history shall be hanged. All the anthologies of African literature destroyed. All the schools of African studies closed down. Ocol becomes surely, in these passages, not a character at all, but an extreme part of the tormented African spirit: the part that, in its despair, would turn from the effort of knitting past with present. "Smash all these mirrors," cries Ocol,

> Smash all these mirrors
> That I may not see
> The blackness of the past
> From which I came
> Reflected in them.

So taboos, customs and traditions must be shattered. The women of Africa must be shown that they have taken pride in what is merely grotesque. The men must be shown how derisory their achievements have been, over the centuries:

> A large arc
> Of semi-desert land
> Strewn with human skeletons . . .
> A monument to five hundred years
> Of cattle theft!

This Ocol—the Ocol of the first half of his song—is driven by a destructive dread and hatred of his African self. And later in the poem, his desire to efface Africa is given a monumental wildness of utterance:

> We will uproot
> Each tree
> From the Ituri forest
> And blow up
> Mount Kilimanjaro,
> The rubble from Ruwenzori
> Will fill the Valleys
> Of the Rift,
> We will divert
> The mighty waters
> Of the Nile
> Into the Indian Ocean.

But from the sixth section of the poem onwards,

the whole nature of the statement seems to change. Now Ocol is one of those who have done well out of Uhuru. In the sixth section, with guilty defiance, he taunts the poor and dispossessed with an account of his properties—

> Do you see
> That golden carpet
> Covering the hillside?
> Those are my sheep . . .

and denies his responsibility for the poverty of the peasantry. And from now on, we are not sure how to take the voice of Ocol. He speaks at times in terms of an ironical observer regarding him from outside.

> We sowed,
> We watered
> Acres of Cynicism,
> Planted forests of Laughter,
> Bitter Laughter . . .
> Fat Frustrations
>
> Flourished fast
> Yielding fruits
> Green as gall . . .

Those who stand aside from this fearful opportunism are "cowardly fools"; they must creep back and hide in their mothers' wombs. And in the eighth section there is another change in the voice—or another note enters briefly and confusingly into it. For a moment

Ocol speaks with something like tenderness of the world he once shared with Lawino:

> That shady evergreen *byeyo* tree
> Under which I first met you
> And told you
> I wanted you,
> Do you remember
> The song of the *ogilo* bird
> And the chorus
> Of the grey monkeys
> In the trees nearby?

But from this unexpected wistfulness Ocol turns at once to a fiercer fury than ever. He tells Lawino that there are only two alternatives:

> Either you come in
> Through the City Gate,
> Or take that rope
> And hang yourself!

The City is barely described. It is defined almost entirely by negation—by an account of what must be destroyed to clear the way for it.

And as an end to the poem there is a last storm of wildly ironical self-disgust. The monuments in the modern Africa will be effigies of its founders: Leopold of Belgium, Bismarck. Streets will be named after the European explorers. All the great men of the African past were made nothing by defeat and irrelevance.

> What proud poem
> Can we write
> For the vanquished?

A final question that makes it impossible not to remark to oneself that such a proud poem has certainly been written, and by Okot p'Bitek: and that it was called *Song of Lawino*.

Song of Ocol, as fierce and powerful as anything Okot has published, seems to me very much a poem in which the author is moving towards a new position. I mean that it begins as a statement that, in the extreme violence of the view it expresses, must make it an expression of the impulse in a modern African to raze his whole world flat and begin again. Ocol, whom we had taken even at Lawino's worst estimation to be a new young African of a fairly characteristic type, turns out to be a sort of super-Tamburlaine, in his destructiveness, driven by an almost hysterical dread of the black past and much of the black present. Clearly, Okot is no more expressing the whole of his self here than he was in *Lawino*. It doesn't begin to be a personal statement: it is the ferociously extreme utterance of something that is in the African air. But the poet cannot keep this up: because the destructive, desperate Ocol is also one of those who have turned Uhuru into an opportunity for their own advancement. So the end of the poem, its second half, is an attack, by ironical implication, on those who have betrayed the hopes that fed the fight for independence. By the end of *Song of Ocol,* it seems to me, Okot p'Bitek has moved into the position that made possible the writing of this new sequence of poems, *Song of a Prisoner*. Certainly, to turn from his first long published poem to these last ones, he had to swivel: from teasing impersonations to impersonations that are deadly serious: from the "lightness" of which Taban lo Liyong has spoken to an unsmiling gravity. The distance between *Lawino* and *Song of a Prisoner* is, I feel, in some respects so great that added force is given to lo Liyong's suspicion that the earlier poem was in essence very early indeed.

"Only rarely," lo Liyong wrote of *Lawino*, "do I see an Okot with tight lips and protracted visage." That a friend who knew him so well should have looked for such an Okot, and should have based so much of his criticism of Lawino's lament on that Okot's absence, does suggest that between the jester and the more serious man an acute struggle may long have been going on. The fact is that *Song of a Prisoner* is throughout a work of the tightest lips, the most protracted visage. The jester has vanished; though not the user of masks. In *Lawino* and *Ocol* Okot spoke—as we have seen, with bafflingly variable degrees of convincingness—through the mouths of his characters. Much of the voice of Lawino must have been his own: and, one feels, even in its desperate extremism, something of the voice of Ocol. In this new sequence, Okot dons several such masks. The prisoner cannot be read as a single character. At times he is a kind of Patrice Lumumba, being beaten to the point of death: a betrayed hero of Uhuru.

At other times he seems to be any political detainee, imprisoned for his opinions or his political actions. Again, he is an assassin, who has rid his country of a tyrant: who pretends wildly not to understand why his captors do not form a guard of honour for him.

We see, from the dedication, that the sequence is wide-spread in its reference. It makes two major statements: both familiar to us, though not in such agonised tones, from *Song of Lawino*. The first is that the hopes of Uhuru have been wrecked, and horribly. The state of a newly independent African country may be even worse than before, since it is worse to be devoured by your own people than by strangers. The second statement is barely a statement at all . . . rather it is a constant reference to a dream. As Lawino looked back at the vision of Acholi order and comeliness of life, so the prisoner constantly sets up a dream of peaceful happiness:

> I have bought
> A farm
> In the fertile valley,
> A thousand acres
> Of heaven
> For you and me
> And our children,
>
> The crested cranes
> Dance love dances
> By the stream
> That flows gently

> Through our garden,
> Our children will play
> And swim in the stream
> And hook fish
> For the afternoon meal . . .

It is the tone of Lawino's celebration of the good things in the Acholi way of life. And added to this is the longing for old prides, old understandings. The assassin yearns to go back to his village, to be received there as one who has killed from a necessity generally understood, to be cleansed and to be marked with the killer mark. It seems to me, I must say here, as widely off the point to claim that, in such passages, Okot is crying for a return to an older Africa as to make such a claim for his arguments in *Song of Lawino*. It is a hearking back, rather, to the past, not as a pleasing mode of life, but as an experience on which some decent order had been laid: when there were recognised ways of setting a limit to the larger tyrannies, the more intolerable greeds. In the light of this sequence, I do not see how one can continue to have any doubt as to the import of Okot's backward looking. It is, in a sense, a metaphor for a kind of forward looking—for a looking, at any rate, in any direction but towards the spectacle of modern Africa as the prisoner experiences it: where

> Black corpses stream
> Along the streets,
> Dead to free Africa

> So that they may
> Suffer in
> Freedom!

And to these elements we must add another. There is a great cry, at many points in these poems, but most clearly towards the end of the sequence, for a sort of vast international tolerance—a relaxed international order. The prisoner wants to dance all the dances of the world, to sing all the world's songs. He wants even

> to dance the dances
> Of colonialists and communists . . .

Even, that is, to span the widest gulfs of ideology and political action. There is a great weariness in this sequence of all the waste of human strife.

For all the changeableness of the masks behind which the poet sings his desperate songs, *Song of a Prisoner* seems to me a true sequence, as some series of poems so linked do not succeed in being. It is held together, of course, in the first place, by the pure style of the poet. There is much here that readers of *Lawino* will recognise—given the far grimmer context. There is, above all, and even more cunningly and evocatively used than before, the constant reference back and forth to the life of animals, insects, plants. These references are methodically placed in the sequence, so that no human event is without its gloss drawn from nature. Again, the images may be used to suggest a deceptive simplicity and sweetness, a sort of hopeless happiness: sometimes, as in *This Stupid Bitch* and *Voice of a Dove,* the references to animals (in both these cases, to birds) give to the opening a soaring pleasantness that makes all the fiercer the descent into the prison, the actual *use* made of the image. I am struck, in many of these passages, by the absence of all strain, the effortlessness, with which Okot modulates into lyricism. He has always been a poet who seems to sing with ease: it is hard to find a phrase in his work behind which you can detect any large pretension. So with:

> The yellow acacia thorn tree
> Lifts up her arms,
> Her clean fingers
> Speak soft invitations
> To the yellow birds . . .

It may even be careless (a purist might object to the obviousness of the three adjectives in those three lines —I mean, to the obviousness with which each noun is given its adjective). But the lyricism seems always to come at the right—that is, usually, the startling— moment: to sustain this curious weaving, so characteristic of the poetry, of violence and sweetness. And once more, the effect of these images drawn from the common scenes of a continent rich in insect, animal and vegetable life is far more than decorative, or descriptive: again, this is one of Okot's devices for giving the deepest possible roots to his work. And at other times the references to nature are fierce and grim:

> A stone wall
> Of guns
> Surround our village,
> Steel rhinoceroses
> Ruin the crops . . .
>
> I am an insect
> Trapped between the toes
> Of a bull elephant . . .

I am struck always, as I say, by the naturalness of these images, in the sense that they arise in Okot's text with a kind of inevitability. Never behind such images was there less feeling of a mere search for colourfulness. But then, Okot can indeed—and I suppose it is partly the oral tradition that makes this possible for him—employ even a slightly bizarre figure of speech and make it seem natural: as in

> Olympic athletes throw javelins
> Inside my belly.

The sequence is held together, too, by the recurring or echoing themes or passages. So we are constantly in a court of law, or some other place of judgement: so the prisoner, in this of his guises or that, is perpetually being required to plead guilty or not guilty. And always he answers with another plea altogether, until, when the sequence is over, he has pleaded a great range of emotions: fear, helplessness, hopelessness, smallness (how unexpected and telling, that!), hatred . . . It is the entire history of the moods of imprisonment; we are swept through the whole awful landscape of imprisoned despair. And again, a theme to which the earlier poems have accustomed us appears—or perhaps it is rather a note struck than a theme. Lawino spoke so often of the manliness of her clansmen, of the masculinity and athletic pride she felt Ocol had lost. The prisoner's sense of his own fate is made more bitter by the memory of his own virility: he was a footballer and a boxer: he is a man to whom it is natural to compare the pains of hunger with javelins thrown by Olympic athletes. He had teeth that

> were the
> White *okok* birds
> Standing on the back
> Of a buffalo bull.

Beaten by his "uniformed brothers," refused a blessing by "our black nationalistic bishop," aware of wife raped, of children excluded from school and employment—raging against tribalism, capitalism, diseased nationalism—he thinks constantly, intolerably, of the power there once was in his own beaten body.

I spoke earlier of the dark laughter in *Song of a Prisoner*: and I can understand that a reader might claim that he found no laughter in this sequence, at all. I use the word in its very widest reference. It seems to me, for example, that those two companion poems, *Bonfire* and *This Stupid Bitch*—in the first of which the prisoner upbraids his dead, rotting father for choosing such a wife, and in the second of which he attacks his mother for marrying such a husband—a very dark humour is at work, using the mirror argument of these two poems to bear his meaning as to the intolerable character of tribalism, and especially of tribalism wedded to modern politics, which may exclude so many of the beneficiaries of Uhuru from all prospects in life.

In the end, when we have read and thought about these latest poems by this remarkable African, we may be left—and particularly non-Africans may be left—with a sense of having, in a dialectical sense, bitten off more than we can chew. I mean this: that we may feel (and many Africans must feel) we do not exactly know how to evaluate this apparently wide-glancing attack on post-Uhuru Africa. This is no issue, especially for an outsider, to comment upon lightly. We cannot attempt to gather up the entire African experience and to say that on it *Song of a Prisoner* is a meaningful general statement. It is certainly no cue for a widespread disillusionment with independent Africa. All an outsider can say is that, given the disorder which colonialism brought to Africa, given the disorder in which it quitted Africa, it will take patience and nerve to rebuild African stability, and to repair what has been broken. Perhaps only a fellow Ugandan can judge Okot p'Bitek's particular case. In all respects in which it is a sequence of personal poems, it must be left to longer and more intimate judgement than we can bring to it. But *Song of a Prisoner* is, clearly enough, not simply a series of poems of personal experience. It is a song, agonisingly felt, most powerfully expressed, vivid and individual, about the universal experience of political imprisonment.

> How can I think freely
> When the very air I breathe
> Has ears larger than
> Those of the elephant
> And keener than the bones
> Of the *ngaga* fish?

More than Africa speaks there, and to an audience larger than Africa.

I am aware of letting Okot p'Bitek down, rather, in those last words. Of course this is a poem of very explicit personal anguish. Of course no one can doubt that Okot feels himself to be the "proud Eagle, shot down by the arrow of Uhuru." He cries out clearly enough to the "pressmen of the world":

> I want to speak to you,
> For the candle
> Of Uhuru
> Has been blown out . . .

I did not wish to evade this direct challenge of the poet's: but only, as (to return to the beginning) a modest early mapmaker, not to plunge into judgements of a kind not strictly necessary to a verdict on a poem or a sequence of poems. As a private reader, I have my own way of reading *Song of a Prisoner*. As a public critic, I can only try to account for my admiration of the poems as poems.

But I feel of them much as I have felt about *Lawino*. As I see it, Okot's power as a poet is of the kind that perpetually raises his work above the particular emotions and experiences—necessarily very tangled in any poet, and in him probably most severely tangled—from which it sprang. This is to be a really good poet. I don't believe anyone could seriously think about modern Africa without trying to weigh the meaning of *Song of Lawino* and *Song of a Prisoner*. I believe *Lawino* has an importance far beyond the boundaries of Uganda: it is, when generalised, a poem about the situation in which we all find ourselves, being dragged away from all our roots at an ever-quickening rate. I believe, as I have said, that beyond the note of alarm and anguish that it strikes as to the condition of some newly independent African countries, *Song of a Prisoner* is full of the despair and anger, fiercely expressed, of anyone anywhere who is politically in chains. But having said all this, one is left with a last—and perhaps, in the end, even more important—thing to say. And that is that Okot p'Bitek is a marvellous poet. I wish I could read him in his own language. But in English he has found a tone, a pattern of verse, a rhythm, that are highly original and inventive. It would not be easy to mistake Okot, in English, for anyone else. Though —and perhaps my friend Taban lo Liyong will note this—his matter is never light, his manner often is, in a sense that any writer must envy. I count him among the few masters I have read of literary mischievousness.

He can modulate from one mood to another with a skill that, though startling in its effect, rarely draws attention to itself. He is a master of writing for the human voice—and sometimes, I suspect, for the animal or insect voice, too. Much in his style might be made the basis of an argument for drumming, as a musical accomplishment for a poet, in much the way that one might have said experience of the lute was a formative influence on Elizabethan verse. And finally, Okot p'Bitek, as man and poet, is one of those valuable souls who add manifestly to the gaiety of the nations, at the same time that much of what he expresses is closely concerned with their agony.

EDWARD BLISHEN

May, 1971

1. Dung of Chicken

The stone floor
Lifts her powerful arms
In cold embrace
To welcome me
As I sit on her navel,

My head rests
On her flat
Whitewashed breasts,

She kisses
My bosom
My neck
My belly button
My back
My buttocks
And shoots freezing bullets
Through my bones,

That giant firefly
On the high ceiling
Rains fiery hailstones

Into my closed eyes
Punching holes
Through the thatch,

There is a colourless rainbow
On the bleak white walls
And on the brow
Of the weeping stone floor . . .

.

Do you plead
Guilty
Or
Not guilty?

.

I plead drunkenness,
I am intoxicated
With anger,
My fury
Is white hot,
My brain is melting,
My throat
Is on fire,

I am dizzy
With frustration,
I am drowning
In the deep Lake
Of hatred,
My heart is riddled

With the arrows
Of despair,
My head is bursting . . .
Oh!

.

See the muscles
Of my arms,
I can break your neck,
Do you realise that?
Do you know
I was a footballer
And a boxer?
I have been a wrestler
And a runner,
I am a great hunter,
I have killed three buffalos
And a hippopotamus
Single handed . . .

.

Look at the laughing wound
In my head
Its cracked negro lips
Painted with dirty brown ochre,

Do you see
The beads of blood
On my legs and feet?
My nose
Is a broken dam,

Youthful blood leaps
Like a cheetah
After a duiker,
Two fingers
The width of the new gap
In my teeth . . .

   .

Brother,
How could I
So poor
Cold
Limping
Weak
Hungry like an empty tomb,
A young tree
Burnt out
By the fierce wild fire
Of Uhuru,

How could I
Inspire you
To such heights
Of brutality?

Brother,
I am not a witch,
I was not caught
Dancing stark naked
Around your house,
Did you find me

In bed with your wife
Or raping your mother?

Why should I not
Sleep with the green grass
In the City Park
While I nurse
My hunger?

Why do they call me
A vagrant
A loiterer?

.

Your Honour,
Why do they beat me
With their clubs
And tie my hands
And feet
With this rope?
Why do they box
And slap me?
Why do they ram my feet
With the butt
Of their rifles?

Your Honour,
Why do they
Punish me
Before I plead

Or am found
Guilty?

   .

The dark silence
Urinates fire
Into my wounds,
The hollow laughs
Of my uniformed Brothers
Fan the fire,
I am engulfed
By a red whirlwind
Of pains
Hotter than the pangs
Of childbirth,
More deadly than
The venom
Of the black mamba . . .

   .

My children howl
Like mad dogs,
A lullabye is stuck
In their mother's throat,

My father
Is asleep
In the stomach
Of the earth
Unseeing

Unhearing
Undreaming,

Listen to the footsteps
Of the wizard
Dancing on my father's
Grave?

2. *Wounded Crocodile*

A foul mushroom cloud rises
And clings on the bare walls
Like a baby monkey
On its mother's back . . .

My lungs hurl themselves
Against each other
My heart shouts
And tries to separate them . . .

A volcano erupts . . .
It is the Chief's dog
Barking,
Listen to the echoes playing
On the hillsides . . .

How many pounds
Of meat
Does this dog eat

In a day?
How much milk . . . ?

.

Have you seen
The mosquito legs
Of my children?

A witch
Has sprayed yellow paint
On their heads,
Their infant pregnancies
Are years overdue . . . !

My wife cleans her pot,
Her kitchen fire
Burns gently,
The water simmers . . .

She and her children
Sit and wait
For the beans
Maize flour
And salt
Which I promised
To take home
For lunch!

.

My children's heads
Are bowed down

With heavy sleep,
But their stomachs
Drum sleep off
Their eyes . . . !

.

I plead hunger
Fiercer than a
Wounded crocodile,
Olympic athletes throw javelins
Inside my belly,

A Saharan thirst
Engulfs me,
My tongue hangs out
And I pray to Lazarus,
    Brother Lazarus,
    Please,
        Just a drop . . . !

3. *Black Mud*

Listen to the drizzles
Dancing lightly
On the leaf of the
Olam tree,
Do you hear
The faint rhythms
Of their feet
And of their drums?

Listen to their
Mocking songs
Accompanied by the haughty horns
Of my Brothers' jeers . . .

.

Ten uniformed Stones
Break into my tiny hell,
Elephants trumpet
Rhinos scream
For blood
And charge,

The earth shakes her belly,
The walls jump
And dance,
The stone floor
Urinates
Orgasm . . .

.

Do you plead
Guilty
Or
Not guilty?

.

My mother slashes
The wall of the black sky
With her ululation,
My sister mumbles a dirge
And rolls herself
In the dust,

An alarm is raised,
The war drum rumbles
Like thunder
Over the Lake,
War horns
Pierce the walls
Like bullets . . .

My clansmen
Are gathered

The blades of their spears
And swords
Embrace the faint moonlight
And dance like butterflies
Over the corpse
Of a rat,

The warriors
Push the dark wind
With their buffalo-hide shields . . .

.

Old hyenas
Fight over the remains
Of a Lamb,
They suck
The eyeballs
And tear painlessly
At the tongue,
Penis,
Testicles . . .

.

A stone wall
Of guns
Surround our village,
Steel rhinoceroses
Ruin the crops
In the fields
And sneeze molten lead
Into the grass-thatched huts,

Roaring kites
Split the sky
And excrete deadly dungs
On the heads
Of the people,
Pots and skulls
Crack . . .

.

Do you plead
Guilty
Or
Not guilty?

.

I plead smallness,
I am a mere
Pygmy
Before your
Uniformed Power
Which towers like
Mount Elgon
And covers the Land
With its dark shadow,

My ear drums
Are torn
I cannot hear you,
A red wall
Stands between you
And me,

I cannot see you,
But I feel
The cold blade
Of your axe
On my neck!

I plead fear,
I plead helplessness,
I plead hopelessness,

I am an insect
Trapped between the toes
Of a bull elephant,
I am an earthworm
I grovel in the mud,
I am the wet dung
Of a chicken
On the floor!

The cry of my children
And the sobs
Of my wife
Haunt me like
A vengeful ghost,

The fiery lips
Of my sister's song
Burn me like leprosy,
The hammer of my mother's

Helpless ululation
Bashes my brain . . .

I plead insanity
I am out
Of my mind,
I am
Mad,
Can't you see?

   .

The owls
Keep silence,
Cocks refuse to crow,
Bats clap their wings
Against the black mud
Of the night
In which
The Eagle
Of Time
Is stuck!

And I
Trembling,
Hungry,
Mad,
Sit,
Shit,
Spit,
Hate,
Wait . . .

4. Bonfire

The setting sun
Pours blazing oil
Into the Lake,
The water is covered
With the blood
Of dying hippos,
Crocodiles, fish
And fishermen . . .

.

You
My old man
Rotting in the earth,
What an idiot
You were!

Why did you choose
This stupid bitch
For a wife?

Why did you vote
For this silly girl

To be my mother?
You should have known
The Tribe and the Clan
In which the most intelligent
Hardworking,
Thrifty
Ruthless
And most successful Chiefs
Are born and bred . . . !

Father,
But you were handsome,
Your limbs were powerful,
You were a great dancer:
I inherited my drumming talents
From you. . . .

Why did you
Not elope with a girl
From the right Clan and Tribe?
Why did you not woo her
With your colourful headgear
And the songs of the 'mother drum'?,
Could you not rape
A woman from the
Right Clan and Tribe
And make her pregnant
With me?

Why did you
Not scatter your seeds

In the air
So that the wind may
Plant them in the rich
Black soil of the great
Clan and Tribe?

Do you not know
That offsprings inherit
Intelligence,
Hard work,
Thrift,
Ruthlessness
And success
From their mothers?

.

Listen
You fool,
When I get out
Of this hell,
I will exhume your bones
And hang you
By the neck . . .

I will kick
Your stupid skull
And punish you
For the sins
Of your boyhood days,

I will look
For the grave of

Your father
And dig him up,
I will discover
The grave of your mother
And dig her up,

I will make a big
 Bonfire
And burn your bones
 To ashes . . . !

5. Sacred Rock

The stone floor
Weeps ice tears,
Poisoned thorns
Pierce my naked feet,
The sweating walls
Shoot needles
Into my back
And throw cold insults
At me,

The heavy smell
Of Death
Fills the room
Like darkness,
The alcohol
Of the black silence
Intoxicate me,

There is a carpenter
Inside my head,
He knocks nails
Into my skull,

My feet are a pair
Of pregnant women
Heavy like grinding stones
And full of the fangs
Of the cobra . . .

My penis
Is an elephant's trunk
Vomiting blood
Like a woman
In her moon,

My wife is
The barusus palm
That has fallen
On a dung heap,
Her breasts heave
And whisper a welcome,
She is cold,
She sobs,
Her body rocks
With grief and regrets,

My bed
Is a Lake
Of tears . . .

.

A black Benz
Slithers smoothly
Through the black night

Like the water snake
Into the Nile,
Listen to it purring
Like a hopeful leopard,
Listen to its
Love song,
The soft poem
That embraces the valleys
And caresses the hills . . .

The grasses on
The pathway
Hiss in protest,
The shrubs scratch
Its ribs
With their nails,

Foxes hit the windscreens
With their laughter,
Dogs whine
And sharpen their teeth,
The gods riddle the car
With yellow arrows
Of starlight . . .

.

My bed yells
In rhythm,
Woman giggles
And shrieks
In sweet agony . . .

Man breathes heavily,
Bathes in sticky sweat
And hides his shameless face
Between the large breasts
Of my woman . . .

Big chief
Is dancing my wife
And cracking
My sacred rock!

.

Do you plead
Guilty
Or
Not guilty?

.

I plead
Guilty
To hatred,
My anger explodes
And destroys like a hurricane,
My jealousy is darker
Than the coming storm
And madder than thunder . . .

Cut off this rope,
Free my hands and feet,
I want to chase
The thief,

I will smell him out
And smear the road
With his brain . . .

.

He throws sacks
Of dust
Into my eyes
And deluges me
With a bucket
Of mud,

His spittle covers me
Like dew
And makes me stink
Like gonorrhea,—
He wipes his arse
On my head
And plucks off
All my feathers,
He throws me into a pond,
I shiver
My teeth clatters
While he nestles on the bosom
Of my young wife . . .

.

I want to drink
Human blood
To cool my heart,
I want to eat

Human liver
To quench my boiling thirst,
I want to smear
Human fat on my belly
And on my forehead,

Mix chyme
With goat blood
And I will drink it,
My inside is full of fire
I must drink
Human blood
To cool me down . . .

6. *This Stupid Bitch*

A bird's song
Breaks through the high ceiling,
It is the lady-bird
Collecting nectar
From the banana blossom
And flying back
To her nest,

The chicks
Chirp their thanks
In unison . . .

.

I plead sickness,
I am an orphan,
I am diseased with
All the giant
Diseases of Society,
The walls of hopelessness
Surround me completely,
There are no windows

To let in the air
Of hope!

   .

Mother,
Mother,
Why did you choose
An ugly and ignorant fool
For a husband?

Why did you elect
This poor man
From the wrong Clan
And from the wrong Tribe
To be my father?

Did you not know
The right Tribe and Clan,
The Ones that produce
The most beautiful,
Most powerful,
The cleverest,
And most successful men?

Why were you
In such a rush
To get married
Mother?

But you were beautiful,
Your voice is still smooth

And sweet
Like refined honey,

Could you not
Woo a man from
The right Clan and Tribe
With your song?
Could you not entice him
With the twist
Of your soft waist
And lure him
With your oiled smile
Into the grass?
Could you not
Persuade and encourage him
With your mock refusals?

Mother,
Could you not bribe
Or blackmail
A man from the right Clan
And Tribe
To sleep with you
And make you pregnant?

Do you not know
That children inherit
Beauty,
Power,
Wealth,
Cleverness

And success
From their fathers?

Do you not understand
What heredity
Is?

.

Listen to the song
Of the flies
Feasting on the eyesores
Of the blind beggar,
They call me
A foreign bastard,
They describe my clansmen
As fools and weaklings,
Can you hear them saying
That my Tribe
Will never rise to Power,
And I will die in deep poverty
And my children
Will become thieves?

7. *Voice of a Dove*

The tiny *lagut* bird
Carries a leaf of grass
To the *olango* thorn bush
To erect a hut
For her children
Who knock loudly
At the gate
And scream
To be let out . . .

.

Wife
Wife,
Are you asleep already?
Is my son
Kissing your teats
In his sleep?

Sleep peacefully
My love,
Dream sweet dreams,
Dream about our first meeting
In the forest . . .

When you hear
The Great news
Jump with joy,
Take the battle axe
From under the bed
And dance the war dance,
Cut the earth with the axe
And make ululations,
Rejoice love!

When you hear
I have been arrested
Do not waste
Your kindly tears
Not a sob
Not a shriek,

I will not be hanged,

I will plead
Not guilty,
The best lawyers
Will defend me,
Our black nationalist judges
And those who hired me
Will set me
Free . . .

.

A python enters
Into a dead termite mound

And swallows the edible rat
And all its young,
An ostrich races
Across the dry plain
To cover her eggs
As the storm threatens . . .

.

Wife,
Tell the children
Not to cry for me,
Let them be proud
Of me,
Teach them the war song
About me,
Let them sing it every day,
Let them learn to be proud
And brave
Like their father!

My love,
Sleep for the last time
In that old hut
With the leaking thatch,
Sleep for the last time
On that dirty papyrus mat
On the earth,

I have bought
A farm
In the fertile valley,

A thousand acres
Of heaven
For you and me
And our children,

The crested cranes
Dance love dances
By the stream
That flows gently
Through our garden,
Our children will play
And swim in the stream
And hook fish
For the afternoon meal . . .

Your house stands
On the crest
Of a small hill . . .
Darling,
Your bed is soft
Like the voice of a dove
And warm
Like the womb.

8. Distant Echoes

The *lek* lizard
Wields his deadly tongue
And smashes a mosquito
To death . . .
There are tears of joy
In his eyes!

The sharks of Uhuru
Devour their own children,
The heads
Of their blood brothers
Bash with the battle axes
Of their tails!

I hear
The triumphant song
Of the hero of Uhuru,
Listen to him

Shout his praise name,
Hear his footsteps
As he prances
The mock-fight
Of victory . . .

.

Yes
I did it
And,
My God,
What a beautiful
Shot!
I scattered
His stupid brain
Into a thousand drops,
His proud body slumped
And soiled our Land
With his rotten blood!

.

The crickets whistle
In sorrow,
Young toads leap
In the air
And yell for help,
Mama frogs blow
Cold air
Into their burning throats

And croak their children
To bury their heads
Into the cold mud . . .

.

I am not senseless,
I am not cowardly,
Not dastardly,

I am not a thug,
I am not insane,
This is not
Cold-blooded murder,
I did not do it
For the money . . .

He was a traitor
A dictator
A murderer
A racist
A tribalist
A clanist
A brotherist . . .

He was corrupt
A reactionary
A revisionist
A fat black capitalist

An extortioner
An exploiter . . .

   .

A fat mosquito
Hums a sweet song
And soothes
The snoring sleeper . . .

   .

You uniformed Brothers
Beating me now,
Why do you not
Salute me?
Form a guard of honour
So that I may inspect you,
Let the band play
Heroic tunes
As you march past me,
Shout three cheers
And congratulate me . . .

He was a spy
A dirty dog
Of foreign powers,
A puppet dancing
To the songs of
Imperialist and neo-colonialists,

His stony cruelty
Covered the Land

Like the black darkness
Of the night,
Men choked in silence
Their chests breaking
With unspoken opinions
And unexpressed feelings,

The jails are filled
With men and women
Chained to their beds
Like penned goats . . .

.

The *til* antelopes
Graze on the steep hillside,
The waters of
The swift river
Rush over rugged rocks,
Leaping like young athletes
And singing a new song:
In praise of rain,

Two bulls wrestle
With their horns,
The horn of the ruling bull
Breaks
And he tumbles down
The smooth breast
Of the hill
And plunges
Into the river.

9. Jubilant Throng

A long convoy
Of black ants
Wind their way
Through the wilderness
Bearing their booty,
They return home
To feast . . .
The queen mother
Of the hillock
Weeps alone . . . !

.

You young widow
In black,
How beautiful you are
With those beads of tear
Glittering on your cheeks,
How dignified
The bearing of your
Sorrow ridden body!

Do not blame me
Sister,
Do not be angry with me,
Do not hate me
You true Daughter
Of the Land.

Your husband was
An obstacle blocking
The path of Our Progress,
He had to be urgently removed . . .

I had to kill him,
And I did it kindly,
He did not suffer long,
He died instantly!

He was arrogant
And your beauty spurred him on,
His words were swords,
Heads rolled when he spoke . . .

.

When you embraced
Your man
In your soft bed,
Other wives wept alone
Covered only by the blanket
Of bitter agony,

And taunted by the memories
Of past embraces,

When you sat around
The table
And joked with him,
Other wives sang red dirges
And beckoned the ghosts
Of their murdered husbands,

When you heard his voice
Through the telephone
And saw him on television,
Others played with
The distant echoes
Of dead men's voices,

When you walked hand in hand
By the Lakeside
And let the starlight
Dance on your white teeth
As you smiled and giggled,
Other wives cut
The veins of their neck
To let their black sorrows
Flow out with their blood!

.

My sister,
Do not be angry with me,
Show gratitude to me,

I have done a great thing
I have liberated
The People
And have made You
Famous!

10. *Killer Mark*

Open this steel gate
You uniformed Brothers,
Open the door
And let me out,

Where is your nationalism?
Where your patriotism?
Where is your love
For the Motherland?

Open the door,
I want to go home,
I want to be with my children,
I want to talk with my wife,
I do not want to hang
By the neck
Until I am cold
And dead,

I want to plough the Land
And plant the millet,

The planting season
Will soon pass . . .

   .

Cut off this rope
Free my hands and feet,
I want to go to the church
And receive holy communion,
Our black nationalistic bishop
Will bless me
With the holy water,

I want to go to the village
To perform
The cleansing ceremony,
To deaden the sharp spear
Of the vengeful ghost,
Let the elders gather
At the clan shrine,
Let them spear
A black billy goat
And pour its blood
On the village pathway,
I will step on the blood
And smear it on my feet
As I enter the homestead,

The women will wail
Their welcome,
My mother will spit blessing

On my forehead,
And the Elder
Will cut the killer mark
On my back . . . !

    .

I want to join
The jubilant throng
Gathered at the City Park
Waiting for me,
I want to receive
Their thunderous applause . . .
I want to raise my hands
And acknowledge
Their cheers,

I want to shake hands
With the Saturday morning shoppers
And wave to motorists
And cyclists . . .

Let the People see
The hero
Of Uhuru!

    .

Let Parliamentarians
Rise and honour me,
Let them award me
The highest prize

In the Land,
Let musicians
Compose songs about me,
Let the Chiefs
Organise celebrations
Throughout the Country,

Let the People
Drink and dance,
Let them rejoice,

For
The corrupt dictator
Is dead,
The noose on their necks
Is cut . . .

I have done
A great Deed
And have become
Immortal!

11. Soft Grass

Shhhhh!

Listen,
Listen to the millepede
Whispering a lullabye
To her newly hatched baby,

Do not make noises,
Do not disturb
The sleeping one!

.

Stop it,
Stop it,
I am a minister,
Do you not know me?

Do you not
Recognise my voice?
Have you not heard me

Addressing meetings
Or in the radio?
Have you not seen me
On television?
Have you not seen
My pictures in newspapers
And in books?

.

An earthquake erupts,
The steel door threatens
To tear off and fall on me,
The roofs laugh scornfully
And the bleak white walls
Jeer and cheer . . .

.

Don't touch me
With your dirty hands,
Don't touch me
With those rude clubs . . .
Stop it,
Stop it . . .

.

I hear the brown ants
Shouting war cries
And blowing horns
As they throw back
The first line
Of termite warriors

In the bloody battle
Of the hillock . . .

   .

I am responsible
For Law and Order,
I am responsible
For Peace and Goodwill
In the Land,
I am your minister
You are my officers,
I command you . . .

   .

The yellow acacia thorn tree
Lifts up her arms,
Her clean fingers
Speak soft invitations
To the yellow birds,
One hundred of them
Are gathered . . .

Listen to their bitter chorus,
The protests and curses,

I see them
Shake their heads
And spit with contempt . . .

A young man hurls a stone,
The yellow birds

Scatter in all directions
Leaving one struggling
Uselessly for life,

Listen to the anger
In the song
Of their wings . . .

.

Where is my secretary?

Ring up my wife
And tell her
I am on *safari*
And will not come home
Tonight,

Tell her I will be back
In two or three days . . .
I am sure
I will be free
Next week . . .

.

The Rhinos of Uhuru
Kiss their brothers
In the back,
A fountain of red water
Cools the parched earth

And the scorched leaves
Of grass . . .

   .

Ring up my friend and Clansman,
I want to speak to
The chief of the army,
Ring up all my Brothers
In the army and police,
I want to tell them
That my life
Is in danger,
That our Clan and Tribe
Are in danger,
I want them to look
After my wife and children,
And to make plans . . .

   .

The groans of a Bull
Pour like the waters
Of the Wang-kwar falls*
Flooding the Land!

   .

Where is my gold pen?
I want to write letters
To my children
And send them money,

---

* Murchison Falls on the Nile in Northern Uganda.

I will not tell them
I am here,
I don't want them
To know that I am
A prisoner,
I want them to grow up
Without suffering,
I want them to pass
Their examinations
And get good jobs
And buy land,
Houses,
Cars . . .

I do not want my children
To get shocked,
I do not want them
To feel sad and sorry
And cry for me,
I do not want them to know
That my hands and feet
Are tied with ropes
And I am sitting
On the naked thigh
Of the stone floor . . .

.

There is an empty chair
In the cabinet room,
The occupant is on leave,
He is alone
Buried in the cotton wool

Thoughts of hope
Filled with poisoned needles
Of hopelessness . . .

.

Where is my writing pad?

I want to write
To my parents,
I want to send a fat cheque
To my old mother
And another fat cheque
To my old father . . .

But how can I tell them
That I am shoeless,
That my feet are swollen,
Blistered and bleeding?
How can I tell
My mother that I am
Naked and bruised
All over?
I do not want
My mother to kill herself,
I do not want
My father to die
Of a heart attack . . .

I will tell them
That I am coming home
To see them
Very soon . . .

12. *Youthful Air*

Big chiefs are gathered
At the Embassy,
They click glasses
And exchange winks
With glittering wives
And false smiles
With husbands . . .

.

Wake up
You pressmen of the world,
I want to speak to you,
For the candle
Of Uhuru
Has been blown out . . .

What is Uhuru
When all my thoughts
Are deep and silent rivers
Blocked up by concrete walls
Of fear and black suspicions?

How can I think freely
When the very air
Has ears larger than
Those of the elephant
And keener than the bones
Of the *ngege* fish?

Why are the words I speak
Captured and locked up
In a safe?

Open this steel gate
And let me out,

I want to breathe the air
Of my own choice,
I want to wake up early
Before the morning birds
Begin to sing
And swim in the naked air
Of the dying night,

I want to walk
On the soft grass
Of the *olet* grazing ground
And share the sleepy air
With the cows and goats,

I want to sleep
With the sand

At the sea shore
And expose my belly
To the spears of the sun
And swallow the boiling air,

I want to inhale
The youthful air
By the Lakeside
And intoxicate my lungs
With its alcohol,

I want to cool my head
With the dew
Of the morning grass . . .

Open this door
And let me out,
The darkness in here
Chokes me . . .

.

You waiter
Standing there with the tray,
Bring me a large whiskey,
No ice, no water . . .
I want to drink it clean,
I want to drink
A whole bottle of whiskey
To quench my thirst
For freedom,

I want to drink
And get drunk . . .

I want to drink
With my friends in the bar
And at the night club,
I want to sleep
With experienced prostitutes,

I want to drink
With the peasants
In the fields,
And with the old women
In my constituency,
I want to suck *lacoi* beer
And share the sucking tube
With the old men
Around the fire,

Let the French girl
Bring her sexy cognac
And I will drink it,
I will cover her
With my broken kisses,

Let the Munyoro girl
Bring her sickly *amarwa*
And I will share it with her,
I will touch her unbroken breasts,

I want to drink
The honey beer and *waragi*
And the apartheid wine
From South Africa,
Let the Russians bring
Their red vodka
And I will drink it
With my Chinese friends
And break the glasses
On the walls,

Let the Kikuyu
Brew the *njohi*
And mix it with blood,
I will drink it
And give some to
The gallant forest fighters . . .
I want to drink
All the drinks
Of the world,
I want to meet
All the drunkards
And chat with them. . . .

I want to drink
And get drunk,
I do not want to know
That I am powerless
And helpless,
I do not want to remember anything,

I want to forget
That I am a lightless star,
A proud Eagle
Shot down
By the arrow
Of Uhuru!

13. Cattle Egret

My children gather stars
Into their soft songs
And woo the young moon
With their white teeth,

The moon kisses
My daughter's emerging breasts
And my son's dimples . . .

   .

I plead guilty
To pride,
I was not born to this,
I am a great soul
My mother knows this
My uncle told me so,
And my father was proud
Of me . . .

My children call me
Papa!
They run to me

And fall into my arms,
They sing and dance for me
And play games with me.

.

The testicle of the bell
Knocks hard against
The big round thighs which
Scream in sharp pain,

Tired teachers wipe
The chalk dust
Off their faces,
The school dam bursts
And floods of hungry children
Melt into their mothers' bosoms.

My children are
Not among them,
My children do
Not go to school
My children will
Never go to school,
The teachers' cane
Will never touch
Their buttocks,

They will grow up
With the wild trees
Of the bush
And will be burnt down

By the wild fire
Of the droughts!

.

The proud cattle egret
Flourishes his long
And colourful tail
And dances between his
Wives and chicks . . .

.

Look at my athletic thighs,
My chest was broad
And without a scar,
My teeth were the
White *okok* birds
Standing on the back
Of a buffalo bull . . .

Have you heard me
Playing the mother drum?
Have you seen me
In the dancing arena?

Cut off this rope,
Free my hands and feet,
I want to clap my hands
And sing for my children
So that they may dance,

I want to drum the wall
With my hands,

I want to jump up
And dance . . .

Let me beat the rhythm
Of the *orak* dance,
Let my wife shake
Her soft waist before me
And remind me of our first meeting
At the dancing arena . . .

I want to join the youths
At the get-stuck dance,
I want to suck the stiff breasts
Of my wife's younger sister,
I want to wrestle
With my wife-in-law*
And crush the young grass
Beyond the arena . . .

.

Is today not my father's
Funeral anniversary?

My clansmen and clanswomen
Are gathering in our village,
They sit in circles
In the shades of granaries,
But who will make
The welcome speech?

---

* Sister in Law.

Men drink *kwete* beer,
Women cook goat meat
And make millet bread,
But I am not there
To distribute the dishes
Among the elders!

The priests throw morsels
Of chicken meat,
They squirt goat blood
And pour libations
To the assembled ghosts
Of the dead,
But how can I address
The ghosts of my fathers
From here?

How can they put chyme
On my chest and back?
How can my grandmother
Spit blessing on me?

My age-mates have donned
White ostrich feathers,
They are singing a war song,
I want to join them
In the wilderness
And chase Death away
From our village,
Drive him a thousand miles
Beyond the mountains

In the West,
Let him sink down
With the setting sun
And never rise again!

I want to join
The Death dancers,
I want to tread the earth
With a vengeance
And shake the bones
Of my father in his grave!

14. Oasis

Listen to the sandy tunes
Of the desert song
As it rides the sand dunes
Accompanied by the winds
Singing through the palm leaves,

I want to hold hands
With the Arabs
And dance together
With the Israelis,
We shall dance
By an oasis
And cool our feet and hearts
With the water
Of the oasis!

I want to dance the rumba
And the cha cha cha,
I want to dance the white dances
Of the west
And shuffle my feet
Softly on the polished
And powdered wooden floor,

I want to dance
The dances of yellow men
At sunset . . .
Show me the sword dance
Of the Russians
And I will dance,
I will dance the bamboo
Dance of the Chinese
And the rice dance
Of the Japanese,
I will dance with the
Garlanded Vietnamese girls
In the swamps . . .

.

You deaf Brother
Standing there with a club
In your hand,
Can you not read
My sign language?

Cut off this rope,
Open the steel gate,
I want to dance the dances
Of colonialists and communists,
I want to try the dances
Of neo-colonialists
And African socialists,
I want to dance the dances
Of our friends and
The dances of our enemies,

I want to lift their daughters
To my shoulder
And elope with them . . .

  .

Let the Eskimo play and sing
His snowy song
And I will dance
To its whaley rhythm,

Let the Spanish girls
Snap their song
With their fingers
And I will dance like a cock
Wooing a hen,

Let the Zulu girls
Click their mountain song
With their sweet tongues
And I will join the men,
We will strike the earth
Like the falling meteorite!

Listen to the wailing tune
Of the Indian song,
Listen to the purring drums,
I will touch the earth lightly
Like a butterfly
And twist my limbs
To the piercing rhythm
Of the lyre,

I want to hold
The delicate waist
Of the untouchable goddess
In sari,

I want to touch
The vibrating buttocks
Of the Muganda girl
Dancing the *nankasa*,

Let me strike the beaded navel
Of the *dingidingi* dancer . . .
Let me dance
And forget my sorrow,
Let me forget
That I am jobless
And landless,
Forget that I am hopeless
And helpless,
Let me sweat out my frustrations
And anger,

Who wants to know
That his children
Will never go to school
Will never get a job
Or land
Or cow
Or goat?

Let me dance
And forget!

15. Undergrowth

Who are playing
At the night club
Tonight?

.

The Blacks of America
Pour their souls
Over the Water,

Who can resist
The haughty twangs
Of your guitar
And the fat jabs
On the black piano?

Blast the metal horns,
Suck the sexyphones
With your fat lips,

Let me dance to the cutting throbs
Of your wounded song . . .

   .

Listen to the orphans
Wailing in the
High-life tune,
Listen to the bombs
Bursting in the market place
Scattering neat heaps of yams
And pieces of human bones,
I hear the food planes
Exploding in mid air,
The ash of the food
Fall gently on the heads
Of starving children . . .

Listen to the clash of bayonets
As brother digs into brother's chest . . .

Who are playing
At the night club
Tonight?

   .

The Congo forest
Is on fire,
Listen to the groans
Of the elephants
Vomiting water on their
Burning backs,

Listen to the giraffes and pigs . . .
The hippopotami tear
Through the forest climbers
And undergrowths,

Listen to the hunting drums
And the hunting horns
Mingling with the howls
Of hunting dogs,

See the river of pain
On the face of the singer,
The anguish of rape
Bloodshed and death . . .

Black corpses strewn
Along the streets,
Dead to free Africa
So that they may
Suffer in
Freedom!

A white mercenary
Falling with a spear
Through his liver,
Dying to save Africans
From Africans,

A white nun
Her face white
As death,

Four more Black heros
Waiting their turn . . .

Sing Brother,
Sing,
Cover me with the bile
From your heart,
Pump it out with
Your powerful lungs,
I want to bathe in it
And mix it with mine!

.

Free my hands and feet
You uniformed Stone,
Open the steel gate,
I want to join the dancers
Of the world,
I want to shake my madness
Off my head,
I want to forgive
And forget the past,
I want to forget
As you have, conveniently, forgotten
That I was your body-guard,
That I organised your meetings
And shouted your slogans . . .

I want to forget the scar
On my left arm
Which stopped the club

From squashing your skull,
Let me dance vigorously
And laugh at myself,
Let me forget that
I used to get you girls . . .

.

Open the door,
Chief,
I want to dance
All the dances of the world,
I want to sleep with
All the young dancers,

I want to dance
And forget my smallness,
Let me dance and forget
For a small while
That I am a wretch,
The reject of my Country,
A broken branch of a Tree
Torn down by the whirlwind
Of UHURU.

821 B546s 1971

p'Bitek, Okot, 1931-

Song of a prisoner